Single, Straight Men

SINGLE, STRAIGHT MEN

106 Guaranteed Places to Find Them · · ·

DR. DIANA SOMMERFIELD

ST. MARTIN'S PRESS ♦ NEW YORK

Design by Victoria Hartman

Library of Congress Cataloging-in-Publication Data

Sommerfield, Diana.
  Single, straight men.

  1. Dating (Social customs) 2. Single men—United States. 3. Mate selection—United States. I. Title.
HQ801.S67 1986   646.7′7   86-13515
ISBN 0-312-76381-6

First Edition

10 9 8 7 6 5 4 3 2 1

Start Getting What You Want Out of Life!!

Over the years all sorts of my friends and acquaintances have asked for my help in finding a man. They didn't want just any man, of course. They wanted a man to love, to share things with, and to have a meaningful relationship with. A man willing to make a commitment. A very special man.

It's sort of a hobby of mine—helping people find each other. I like to see people happy. After I became a cultural anthropologist, I also began to scientifically study how women can meet men. And over and over again women have taken my advice and found just the guy they were looking for.

Many things everyone "knows" about finding men are actually not true. Many women make the common mistake of believing the myth that the best place to meet available men is somewhere men go looking for women. That is, in the sort of places and situations that are particularly structured to bring the opposite sexes together. Places like singles' bars and singles' cruises. But those are actually the worst places.

In a singles' bar everyone knows why everyone is there so people get defensive and act superior and uninterested. There's a lot of posturing, of people putting others down. It's unpleasant and unnatural, and it can be embarrassing and emotionally painful.

If you want to get picked up and used, those places are great, but if you're looking for a man to spend time with, to go places with, to share things with, and to build a relationship with, those places are all wrong.

You'll discover in this book how to meet men in pleasant, natural, comfortable settings. Places where people act real, where they open up, talk freely, don't posture.

• | This Book Is Filled with Fun, Free, Easy Ways to Meet Lots of Attractive, Compatible, Available Men

You'll discover all sorts of ways to meet unmarried men of all ages, backgrounds, and interests who are looking for a woman just like you to have a real relationship with.

You can start meeting men today—on your lunch hour—if you wish. It's that easy. That fast. And it's a lot of fun!

You can have your pick of men. You'll never be lonely again. You'll have the time of your life for the rest of your life.

It doesn't matter what you look like or how old or young you are. And it doesn't matter if you're overweight or thin, or short or tall. Whether you're rich and beautiful or not so lucky. None of that matters.

If you go to the places recommended in this book and do the things suggested, you'll meet plenty of interesting, compatible, available men. And some of them will be just right for you. And you for them. It's that easy!

◆ Meeting Men Is Easy If You Know This

If you frequent places where men go because of some special interest they have, you'll just naturally encounter lots of men.

But—and it's a big but—there's the right kind of place and the wrong kind of place. Any place where you buy a specific seat and sit in it is the wrong kind of place. That is, places like professional ball games. Sure there will be lots of fellows around if you go to a baseball, football, or basketball game, but you won't have the chance to meet any of them in a pleasant, natural way. It doesn't matter what the activity is either, since the opera's as bad as a tennis match. If you have to buy a seat, it's the wrong sort of place to meet men easily.

But this book is full of places where men gather in unstructured situations—over a hundred places where there are lots of men whom you can easily meet in a pleasant, natural way.

◆ | All The Recommended Ways to Meet Men in This Book Have Ten Important Things in Common

1. All of them allow you to meet the men face-to-face, because of that wonderful and mysterious, yet difficult to define, thing called chemistry. You'll know right away if a man you meet is "your type."
2. You personally select all the men you meet, so they're all your type.
3. The recommendations are very specific. They tell you exactly where to go, when to go, the sort of men you'll meet, what to do, and even what to say to start a conversation.
4. All the suggested ways to meet men feel natural and comfortable. You'll never be embarrassed, for none of the recommended ways is "obvious." No one—including the men you'll meet—will ever know you're looking for a man.
5. There's always something interesting right at

hand to talk about with the man you've just met. You'll never be tongue-tied and at a loss for a subject of conversation.

6. The ways to meet men recommended in this book are interesting, pleasant, and fun things to do, so even if you don't meet the man you're looking for, you'll enjoy the experience and have a nice time.

7. The suggested ways to meet men cover every hour of the day and night, every day of the week, every season of the year, so any time you want to meet a man, you can. No more waiting for Saturday night. No more waiting at all!

8. All the places recommended for meeting men are easy to leave whenever you wish. You will never feel trapped or embarrassed as you might on a blind date. You don't even need to make up an excuse to leave. Yet if you want to stay at these places, that's just as easy. You can stay as long as you want without feeling uncomfortable.

9. Every woman personalizes the recommended ways to meet her exact specifications. Since you are the one who selects exactly which golf course or volunteer agency or restaurant, you can find exactly the sort of men you want to meet.

10. The recommended ways can be used over and over again. You can't use them up. If five or ten or twenty of them work really well for you, you

can use them again and again for years and they'll still be fresh and they'll still work.

◆| Most of the Recommended Ways Also Have These Things in Common

▶ They cost nothing to try. They're free! In fact, you'll even make money doing some of them.
▶ They don't require you to have special clothes or equipment or training. You can try them at once if you want to.
▶ You won't have to leave the area you live in.
▶ They take very little time. If you have even ten minutes, you can meet a man you want to meet.
▶ You'll have an opportunity to meet a number of men—not just one.
▶ They'll allow you to develop new interests and make your life more exciting.
▶ Some of these activities will even advance your career.

◆| A Word of Warning

Never pretend to be interested in some activity or group that you really think is boring. I certainly don't mean that if you've never tried something, you shouldn't try it. By all means explore it and the men who are involved in it. *Just don't fake an interest that isn't really there.*

Why not, you ask? After all, he'll probably never catch on. But that isn't the point. Don't do it because you'll end up with a man who expects you to be fascinated by something that really bores you. You'll be stuck pretending endlessly. You certainly don't want to spend your weekends at the race track if you'd rather be at an art gallery, do you?

Besides, one day your true feelings and your pent-up resentment will slip out and will harm your relationship.

Also men have interrelated interests and experiences so if this great passion of his bores you so will many other activities he's interested in.

Obviously to have a fulfilling life, you have to meet strangers. But whenever you meet strangers, you should exercise due caution and be aware that in rare incidences problems can occur. So be prepared and let your natural caution and intelligence be your guide as you would when dealing with any new situation.

Go ahead and try the different ways to meet men. Decide for yourself if some particular pastime interests you. You'll probably develop many new interests while trying out the suggestions in this book.

But always be yourself. There are lots of men out there just waiting to meet you and to fall in love with you.

◆ | Diana's Happy Hunting Tips

1. Be yourself. Nothing is as eternally fascinating, exciting and mysterious as a woman being herself.
2. Go places alone when you want to meet a man. It makes it much easier. And more fun!
3. Never look for men in places that are supposedly set up especially for that purpose. Bars, singles' cruises, and dances are not the sort of places to meet the kind of men you want to meet.
4. Never pretend to be interested in something that really bores you. Doing that will only make you unhappy and sabotage any relationship, for unless you and he have some real interests in common and some shared values, you won't really have anything to build a relationship on.
5. Self-confidence in social situations is a learned skill. So just relax and you'll develop the ability.
6. Never take your children along when looking for a man. Give him a chance to know you first.
7. Don't put off selecting a career or advancing in it while you wait for Mr. Right to come along. When you develop yourself and your potential fully, any relationship that follows will be better for it.
8. Don't be a shrinking violet. Men like women who enjoy many things and like to try new

things. Men don't really want a woman who is too eager to please them, nor do they want a very predictable woman. Dare to be the real you. He'll love you for it!

9. Never make men compete for you. Most men hate being forced into a competitive situation over a woman, and those fellows who like it are more interested in beating the competition than in winning you. That certainly doesn't mean you can't have two (or more) men at one time, just don't set it up as a competition.

10. Nothing attracts a man like a smile, or makes a woman look more beautiful.

The 106 Guaranteed Places to Find Single, Straight Men

◆ | Buy Your Groceries After Work

Unmarried men don't usually plan their food buying too carefully or too far in advance so they often end up buying what they need on their way home from work during the week. What a great opportunity for you to meet them!

Where should you shop? Begin by casually inspecting a number of stores near major thoroughfares. Just walk around and look at the men who are shopping there.

But keep in mind that the type of job a man has determines the time he gets off work, so if you're looking for a teacher, shop earlier in the afternoon; an accountant, shop later. The best way to decide the right time for you is to take a walking tour of the store at different hours on a typical workday while you size up the prospects.

Glance in his cart to see if he's buying for one or for a family if you spot a man who interests you, but remember that he could have a roommate or be a single father.

How do you meet him? Now, that's easy. Any question or comment such as, "Hmmm, don't the grapes look good today!" should start the ball rolling. Or how about, if you spot popcorn in his cart, "Hi! Excuse me, but I can't seem to find the popcorn. Can you tell me what aisle it's in?" He may even go help you find it.

◆ | Go to Auctions

Auctions are fun places where you can look over hundreds of men who are busy focusing on something that really interests them. There are all sorts of auctions—unclaimed freight, estate sales, foreclosed property, eighteenth-century paintings, Oriental rugs, stamps, you name it. And each different kind attracts a different type of man.

But don't wait until the day of the actual auction. Be a real insider—go during the inspection days when everyone is milling around and looking at everything. That's when it's really easy to ask of the man who's caught your eye, "Do you think that's genuine?" about the item he happens to be looking at. Or perhaps, "What do you think it will go for?" You get the idea.

Look in the newspapers, especially on Saturdays, for advertisements announcing auctions, or look in the Yellow Pages for auction houses and companies that conduct auctions. Then call and find out how to get on their mailing lists.

◆ | Browse in Men's Wear

Since unmarried men have to buy their own clothes, you'll find them in the men's wear department on the weekends and on weekday evenings. Conveniently, different types of stores and different departments within large stores cater to different ages, classes, and types of men, so the men come "pre-sorted" for you! How considerate.

Should you spot a man who interests you while you're browsing, casually go up to him with an article in hand (like a sweater) and say, "Can you help me? I don't know my brother's (father's, son's, nephew's) size, but I think he's probably the same size you are. May I ask what size you'd wear in this?" Obviously, don't say husband, lover, or boyfriend!

◆ | Visit the Library

Ah, the joys of reading and of meeting men who love to read!

All libraries have public reading rooms. In fact some even have comfortable lounge chairs nestled around a roaring fire in a fieldstone fireplace where people can relax with a good book. What a romantic place to meet someone special!

If you live or work near a library or pass one on your way home, drop by regularly and see who's sitting in the reading area. Snowy and drizzly nights are especially good.

Then when you spot a man who looks interesting, snatch up a book of your own and sit down near him. That way—after a while—you can look over at him and say, "Hi. Is that author any good? I've been thinking of reading one of his books myself."

◆ | Take a Night School Course

Just reading the catalog of classes at a college or at a high school that offers night extension classes will whet your appetite. But while you're trying to decide, remember that it ought to be something that truly interests you and that also interests men.

A friend of mine chose furniture making. The class consisted of her and eight guys. One of them —a handsome, blond accountant—is now her boyfriend. Needless to say, she loved the class!

But what if it turns out there's no man in the class who interests you? There's a very simple way for you to up the odds tremendously in your favor. The best strategy—and I highly recommend it—is to do some prospecting. That is, carefully look through the course offerings and select three or four classes that interest you. Then on the night of the first class meeting, drop by all four classrooms and take a look at the available men in each class. The closer it is to class starting time the more of them will already be there. Then choose your course.

Or if the classes that interest you meet at different times or on different days, attend the first sessions of all of them. That'll certainly give you the information you need.

♦ | Volunteer in a Hospital

When you were a little girl, did you use to fantasize about becoming a nurse and falling in love with a doctor or one of the patients? The good news is that you don't have to be a nurse to have this happen. Hospital volunteers read to patients, write letters for them, or just visit them and cheer them up.

It's very rewarding work, for you're filling a very human need and really being of service. And the best part is that any man who meets you will think of you as a ministering angel. This goes for doctors as well as attractive male patients! After all, men had childhood fantasies, too.

This approach works! A friend of mine met Mr. Right this way. By the time he was discharged, she already knew his family and friends who had come to visit him and they all loved her, too.

◆ | Stock Up

Combine learning about investments and financial planning with meeting a man. Free seminars on money management that are offered by brokerage houses and financial service companies are great places to meet men. These seminars are usually held at hotels or other public meeting places such as conference rooms in public libraries. They are by invitation only and you need a reservation, but they are free.

So how do you get invited? You may receive an invitation in the mail or read about such a seminar in the newspaper, but if you don't, call various brokerage firms, especially the big ones, and ask if they are sponsoring any investment seminars. They'll immediately invite you to the next one. Do the same thing with financial service companies. Find them in the Yellow Pages.

Don't worry if you don't know very much about stocks and bonds and government funds and IRAs, TSAs, Keoghs, and Rollovers. You'll learn about them at the seminars, although, of course, the sponsors are also trying to sell you their professional services. But it's not high pressure selling.

When you arrive at the seminar, don't immediately take a seat. Instead, stand by the door, or talk to the host, or just wander around the room. You're waiting to see the men who come in so you can decide whom you want to sit next to.

Since there's usually a question and answer period, you can also get a number of men to notice you by asking questions. Just be sure to stand up and mention your name before you ask the question. Something like, "I'm Judy Edwards, and I was wondering . . ." That way the men will know your name and feel free to approach you after the session and talk to you.

◆ | Visit the Park

You'll find if you go to the park on a Saturday or a Sunday afternoon, most of the kids there will be accompanied by their fathers, for dads often take their kids to the park on their weekly visitation day. So if you've got kids of your own, on this one you can bring them along.

Although most divorced fathers want their children to enjoy themselves and not to wreck their apartment (hence the park), most dads are pretty bored at the park watching their kids swing and climb on the monkey bars. So the man you want to meet will probably be delighted if you sit down on the bench beside him and ask, "Is that adorable little boy your son?" He's likely to fill up with fatherly pride and tell you all about it.

♦ | Attend Golf Tournaments

You don't have to play golf to enjoy a golf tournament. The sky's blue, the grass is green, the air's as soft as velvet and you're surrounded by droves of handsome men.

Unlike other spectator sports where you buy a seat and have to sit in it, there are no seats at golf tournaments. The fans either follow the players around the course or they station themselves at one green and watch all the action that happens at that hole.

The crowd is always moving, shifting, milling, which gives you a perfect opportunity to end up standing right next to the man you want to meet. If smiling at him doesn't do it—it may, since women are not in abundance—just make a comment to him about one of the pros' last shots. "Wasn't that a great putt!"

But take a tip from me—if you know absolutely nothing about golf, watch a tournament on television first before going to one. The commentators on television describe the action and the golf pros so well, you'll feel like an expert in no time. After all, you want to be able to talk to the man once you've met him.

◆ | Hang Out the Old School Tie

If you attended a college or university, you can meet men you'll probably enjoy knowing by joining your alumni association and attending events it sponsors.

If you live in the area where the college is located, you'll probably be invited to a lot of different kinds of events once you join the association. Things like football pep rallies and the homecoming game. Go —men like football. Or it may sponsor a series of lectures or informal discussions by professors, or weekend trips, or dances.

If you don't live in the area, don't let that stop you. Larger schools have branches of their alumni associations in most major cities. If they don't, you can start one in your area.

The local group you join will probably sponsor social events, for the purpose of such groups is to help members meet each other. They may also have a newsletter. See to it you get written up in it as a new member, for old college boyfriends you'd like to see again may very well also belong to the group.

If there is no local group and you decide to start your own, your college will help you by supplying the names, addresses, and phone numbers of the alumni who live in your area. What an opportunity for you! You'll meet a lot of men contacting these people—and they'll know other grads who live in the area. It can really snowball!

◆ | Wash Your Clothes on Saturday Morning

But do it at the laundromat. Scads of single men of all types, ages, backgrounds and interests wash their clothes there from nine till noon on Saturday. Look inside through the big windows as you pull up in your car to make sure this particular laundromat is a "happy hunting ground." If not, drive on to another one. They're listed in the Yellow Pages.

◆ | Go to a Museum

There are all kinds of museums so select one whose subject interests you, for that way so will the men you meet there.

Military museums often have many male visitors as do historical and art museums. But then again some men are interested in furniture, or archaeology, or space exploration, or musical instruments, machinery, or primitive people.

How do you meet him? It's easy. Just "accidently" end up standing next to him and make a comment on whatever he's looking at.

If that approach seems too bold for you, you can try simply catching his eye and smiling. Or you can ask him a question. Something like, "Do you know where the Ming vases are?"

• | Kick Some Tires

I know what you're thinking—you don't want to talk to any used car salesmen.

I'm not suggesting you do. The men I'm suggesting you meet are the other possible buyers for the new and/or used cars you're looking at.

Go on a Friday night or a Saturday morning to a new or used car lot and look over the men who are slamming doors and kicking tires.

Men love cars. Men love to talk about cars. Men like to show off whatever knowledge they have about cars. So why not ask the man you want to meet what he thinks about the car he's looking at?

If you have any knowledge about cars yourself, don't hesitate to use it. Ask intelligent questions. State some informed opinions. But also ask his advice.

• | Volunteer to Help a Political Candidate Get Elected

This is one sure way to meet men from morning till night. You'll meet fellow campaign workers, politicians, voters, and all sorts of media and public relations people. It's exciting and allows you to do some good while trying your hand at things you don't normally have the chance to do, such as writing press releases.

But if they try to make you type, stuff envelopes, and make coffee all the time, remember you're a volunteer so just politely tell whoever is in charge the sort of work you'd really rather be doing. Point out the talents you have that are not being utilized to help the candidate get elected. You're not going to meet many interesting men typing all day.

◆ | Go to a Show

A friend of mine never misses a boat or auto or recreational vehicle show, and maybe you shouldn't either. They're great places to meet men.

These shows are normally held every year at a major auditorium or convention center and feature the latest in cars or boats or campers. Various manufacturers set up displays and exhibits of their wares along aisles, while hordes of men pay a couple of dollars admission to look over, touch, and fantasize about owning the latest trimaran, exotic sports car, or motor home. Some of these shows are huge and attract men from fifty miles around.

Single men especially like these sorts of shows, for the goods on display are just the kinds of things they like to buy for themselves and can afford.

It's easy to find out about these shows, for they're

commercial ventures that advertise in the newspaper. Or you can call the convention center or auditorium in your area and ask them what shows they have booked. They'll be happy to tell you what's coming and when, and to put your name on a mailing list for advance announcements.

◆ | Go Out Looking for a Roommate

Sitting at home bored some Saturday afternoon? Read the classified ads and call up the men who are looking for roommates.

If one of the fellows you talk to sounds promising, go over and have a look at the place and at him.

◆ | Show Newcomers Around

If you work for a large firm, there probably are newcomers who recently moved to your city or out-of-town guests who are affiliated with the firm. These people would really appreciate being shown the sights and given a helping hand if, for example, they are looking for housing. So volunteer.

Although you'll probably have to do at least part of it on your own time, your appreciative firm may pick up your expenses—including nice meals—and probably give you some time off from work.

It's a nice way to make new friends and to be the first woman who meets the just-arrived bachelor.

◆ | Assist Public Television

The educational channel in your city needs view-
ers' contributions to stay on the air. Volunteer to
help with the phones during the pledge drive. That
way you'll be able to talk to a number of interesting
men on the phone, and you will meet men who have
also volunteered to help. You may even be seen on
television answering the phone. The sight of you on
television may make a man who already knows you
suddenly see you in a new light.

◆ | Rewrite Your Resumé

Career planning workshops are excellent places
to meet men, for many men who are thinking of
changing jobs, or who are unemployed, attend
them.

The best career workshops are those that are held
as public services by local colleges or state employment agencies, for they're free and usually very
helpful. So call up your local college—community
or junior colleges like to sponsor these—and check
with your state's employment department.

You do have to register ahead. Usually you have
to bring your resumé, but that's about it. You don't
have to be employed. Nor do you have to be actively
looking for a different job. The sessions are nor-

mally very informal so people easily meet each other.

◆ | Wait in Line

It doesn't matter where you wait in line as long as the man directly in front of you in line is someone you'd like to meet. So when you go to the movies, wait for a bus, or line up at a cafeteria, be selective! Spend a few minutes waiting and watching before you join the line.

Okay, you're in line and he's right ahead of you. Now what? Ask him if he'll please save your place in line for a minute. Of course he'll agree. Now duck out. When you come back, thank him for doing you the favor. If you've had good eye contact while you've been talking to him, the conversation should just flow from there.

◆ | Become an Interested Spectator

Men adore an audience. When you see a pick-up ball game of whatever sort, be it baseball, softball, soccer, football, or basketball, stop and watch and applaud a good performance. A home run. Or a touchdown. An electrifying basket. Clap. Cheer. Wave. Shout out, "Good going!" Whatever feels comfortable for you.

You can stand on the sidelines or sit on the grass

in the shade, but make sure that you're close enough to the players so that if the man whose performance you've cheered wants to come over and talk to you he easily can.

A little bolder, but even better, is to sit down beside the fellow you'd like to meet and compliment him on his performance.

◆ | Give a Company Party

Most companies have annual Christmas parties and picnics in the summertime. Why not volunteer to arrange these parties? It's fun, it'll get you away from your desk, and you'll meet lots of men—at the party and before.

Since you are acting on behalf of your company, you have the opportunity to approach any man who works there and ask for his help. Be creative. Find things you need done. Ask that handsome fellow in accounting you've been wanting to meet if he knows of any good bands. Or of a good caterer.

You'll also be the person who will be talking to the vendors, so you'll get to meet the men who will be supplying the food and drink and decorations, etc., for the big event.

At the function itself, you'll be in charge of over-seeing everything, so assign yourself a seat at the head table near the big boss. It'll be a great chance for you to get noticed by him and all the men who hang around him. The professional benefits of this maneuver may even outweigh the personal, since your administrative and organizational skills will be on display for every level of the company to see.

◆ | Show Off Your Form

Remember how much fun ice skating was when you were young and how you used to meet boys at the rink when you were a teenager? You still can.

Divorced fathers who have their children for the weekend often take them to ice skating rinks during the winter. It's the perfect place, for they have fun and get some physical exercise, and it doesn't cost anything. Money's often a problem for divorced dads.

You might want to suggest that the man you meet and his children come over to your place for some hot chocolate and cookies after the skating is over.

◆ | Deliver Food

If you would like some extra money, consider getting a part-time job making deliveries for the local deli or pizza parlor in the evening. During the Monday night football games you're likely to make deliveries to a number of groups of men who are watching the game. Men playing poker on Friday and Saturday night also get ravenously hungry.

Remember though that these are "guys only" activities so they won't ask you to stay and have a beer. Besides you're working!

But you will meet a lot of men who are in a relaxed and jovial mood and because you'll be the only woman there, you'll certainly stand out in the crowd. And they'll certainly know how to get in touch with you later.

◆ | Visit a Ski Lodge

If you already know how to ski, you've already discovered how many men love downhill skiing. Hearty, athletic men.

But maybe you don't know how and you're wondering if skiing is for you, since a broken arm or leg is not your cup of tea.

The best way to find out if the men and the sport interest you is to go to one of the lodges on a snowy winter afternoon and just sit by the roaring fire and sip something hot.

Smell the air, walk around a bit, sit and think in front of the leaping flames. Since everyone will assume, if you are dressed in skiing attire, that you just came in off the slopes or are about to go out, you can join the skiing scene without ever taking one lesson or even renting a pair of skis! Or ever buying a single lift ticket. You can quite simply try it and the men on for size before you decide.

But maybe you're like me. You decide you like the men but not the sport. I freeze quickly. So what do you do? You spend your time sitting by the roaring fire sipping a rum toddy and never, ever go near the slopes. You meet plenty of men that way.

Just don't pretend to be a skier. You don't want to be a fraud. If someone asks, just admit that you love the ambience of the sport but not the sport.

◆ | Visit the Space Center

You can combine a fascinating tour with meeting lots of men if you visit the Kennedy Space Center at Cape Canaveral in Florida. Since the Space Center is only a short drive from Epcot and Disney World, you might want to go there on vacation or stop by if you're near there on a business trip.

Since men love machinery, adventure, and deeds that require guts and determination, they love touring the Space Center. At the Visitors' Center there are two bus tours. Take both of them, for they're fascinating and both times there'll be lots of men.

It's really easy to meet your fellow passengers, for the bus keeps stopping at interesting places, like rocket launching pads, and everyone gets out and mills around so it's an excellent opportunity for you to strike up a conversation.

And don't miss the exhibits in the museum at the Visitors' Center either.

◆ | Be a Star

Do you have a secret ambition to be an actress? All you have to do is join a local theater group.

Most colleges and universities have these groups and so do many cities and suburbs.

Unless you're extremely lucky you won't start out in a starring role, but it doesn't really matter. You'll be on stage and a lot of men you meet will think you're really special just because of that!

◆ | Catch a Ferry

How about a shipboard romance at a price you can easily afford? Instead of a week's cruise to the Caribbean, spend a day on a ferry boat.

I'm talking about the kind of ferry boats that cross major bodies of water—such as the Great Lakes or those that sail from Maine to Nova Scotia or from Seattle to Victoria, B.C. The crossing might take from four to twelve hours one way.

Since these are normally car ferries, you just drive your car on board, park and leave it, and spend the voyage up on the passenger decks, where there are likely to be restaurants, coffee shops, gifts shops and stores, even bars, entertainment lounges, and sometimes gambling parlors. They also have open decks lined with deck chairs for sunbathing. Plus mobs of people enjoying themselves and the sea.

Taking a ferry ride is so much fun that many people go round trip, staying only a few hours in the port before returning to their original destination. In fact, special reduced price tickets are sold for this very purpose.

• | Ride a Bike

Remember how much fun riding a bike was when you were young? Well, it's even more fun as an adult. Dust off your skills and rent a bike by the hour in a historic area, in a park, or near a lake. For you see, wherever bikes are for rent there'll be single men riding them.

Riding is fun and good exercise and you can wave at all the other riders you pass.

• | Attend Art Gallery Openings

Being interested in the arts can improve your social life as well as your mind. When a new exhibit is opened, a gallery normally throws a party. If painting or sculpture interests you and you're looking for a man who shares that interest, this can be a good bet.

Since these parties are usually by invitation only,

it's best to select a few galleries that you like and drop around regularly and get to know the proprietors. That way, you'll soon start getting invited.

Galleries are also just good places to meet people because they're usually small and cozy and men there often feel like chatting.

♦ | Get Interested in Our Nation's History

Many men are interested in places of historical interest, and the federal government does an excellent job of maintaining many of these areas so the public can enjoy visiting them.

So whether it's Bunker Hill or Antietam battlefield or Fort Kerney or the Alamo, when you go to a place where our nation's history was made you are likely to encounter men who are fascinated by the events that occurred there. And they'll probably be delighted to get into a conversation with you, about the place and its history.

Since the Park Service has set up all sorts of educational displays, shows movies, and hands out maps right there on the spot, you can quickly become informed about the place and the events that occurred there. And usually everything's free!

How do you find these places? Look on maps or in standard guidebooks for the locations. Or write to the National Park Service. The sites are located all over the country. Some are near you.

◆ | Visit a Marina on the Weekend

If you like boats, you're in good company. A lot of men are crazy about boats, so the marina is the natural place to meet them.

Since a lot of men will be talking to each other and looking at each other's boats or working on their own, it's usually easy to start a conversation. Just ask any question of any man.

◆ | Cut Your Hair

Great places to meet men are unisex hair cutting establishments that don't require appointments. You just walk in, put your name on the list, and are waited on by the next available stylist.

Check out a number of these establishments. If you work in an area where many are located, do this on work days, for most men have their hair cut during working hours.

◆ | Share Your Talent

If you're an accomplished musician or singer, let it be known far and wide. Tell friends, ministers, caterers, and wedding photographers that you'll be happy to perform—for free—at anniversaries, weddings, parties, whatever.

If you don't charge for your services, you'll be in great demand and you'll be invited to attend the functions you perform at as a guest as a way for the host or hostess to say thank you.

You'll get to meet all the male guests at the affairs, and all of them will already know your name and that you are the lovely lady who plays the guitar and sings folk songs.

◆ | Volunteer to Be a Coach

You don't have to be particularly athletic or great at sports to coach a child's team. Be it soccer, softball, or swimming—all you need is the interest and the spare time.

If you have a child of your own, you might want to coach the team he/she is on, but that's not necessary. In fact, you needn't even have children of your own to volunteer. Coaches are always needed for the younger children's teams, so call up a local school and volunteer your talents.

So whom will you meet? The kids' fathers and their friends, who'll come to the practice sessions and to the games. Sure some of the dads will be married, but from what I've seen, more divorced fathers go to games and practice sessions than married dads.

You'll also meet the fathers of the players on the opposing teams. And the other coaches—many of whom will be male if you're coaching a boys' team. You'll also meet the officials and the school athletic personnel.

In fact, you'll meet all kinds of men and it's great fun!

◆ | Browse in a Hardware Store

Millions of men are hardware junkies. Gadget nuts. Tool jocks. They love to buy and own tools. Where will you find them? In the hardware stores obviously—ogling the merchandise. Looking at the latest sprinkler connectors, screw drivers, hacksaws, mallets, and the most up-to-date power tools. Walk through a hardware store on any Saturday and you'll see wall-to-wall men.

◆ | Don't Let Him Get Away

What if you're walking down a street and you suddenly see a man ahead of you that you'd just love to meet? Don't miss meeting him.

Go up to him and ask him for one of the two foolproof things you can ask any stranger in America: the time or directions. Make eye contact when you ask.

Then, after he's helped you, offer him your hand

to shake and say, "Thanks a lot. I'm Jenny Michaels." He'll tell you his name and you're on your way!

◆ | Visit the Pro Shop on Saturday

If you're interested in golf, consider how many men stop by the pro shop at the golf course or the country club on Saturday afternoon. So maybe you should too?

A friend of mine volunteered to help out at the pro shop on the day of the annual tournament. She reports, "I have never met so many guys in one hour before!" Although she couldn't remember all their names, they seemed to have no trouble remembering hers.

If you become a regular at the pro shop, pretty soon you'll know a lot of people and you may well get asked to play a round of golf with the man you were hoping to meet.

◆ | Eat Lunch Where the Men Are

What kind of man would you like to meet? A lawyer? An architect? An electrician? A professor? Whatever he does for a living, he eats lunch. And men usually eat in places near where they work. So look in the Yellow Pages to find out the areas of the city where the sort of man you're looking for works, and then drive around those neighborhoods and look for likely places to eat lunch.

As an example, let's say you're interested in meeting a lawyer. Most lawyers have their offices very near the local courthouse so they can get to court easily. So you should start eating lunch in the vicinity of the courthouse.

It's as easy as that!

Since lunch is always a busy time and you usually have to wait for a table, tell the person who takes your name when you enter that you don't mind sharing a table. That way he or she may bring the man you're looking for right over to your table to join you.

◆ | Shoot the Rapids

If you're yearning for a rugged outdoorsman, consider white water rafting. Many of the men who are attracted to this sport seem to see themselves as nineteenth-century mountain men, even if they usually spend their time in an office.

Since many of these trips take three days to a week or even more, and the entire party camps together at night and cooks communally over an open fire, you'll have no problem meeting any man there.

See a travel agent about the trips that are available, but a word of caution. You'll get cold and wet and dirty, so if looking glamorous is important to you, better skip this one.

◆ | Attend Trade Shows

Trade shows are attended by lots of men who are very easy to meet. Everyone wears a name tag! In fact, meeting others is an important reason people have for going to trade shows. In part, people come to make contacts in their field. To build a network.

Trade shows are put on by industries for industry insiders, to showcase the latest products and services that manufacturers are offering in that field. Representatives from companies that supply related products also attend.

Industry associations frequently hold more than one trade show a year and each show normally lasts two or three days. National industries hold them in different parts of the country each time. They usually take place in hotels and convention centers.

Attend trade shows in fields related to yours. And the trade shows of industries you'd like to know more about.

If you inform your boss that you're planning to spend the day attending a specific trade show that's in town, you may actually get points for keeping abreast of new developments in different fields.

So how do you find out about trade shows? Through industry publications—usually magazines devoted to that industry. If you want to go to trade shows of industries other than your own, go to a major library and ask to see its list of publications. Glance through the magazines devoted to your field of interest. Trade shows, their dates, and locations are announced well in advance.

Your Chamber of Commerce can probably tell you which trade associations will be holding shows in your city in the coming year. There's usually an entrance fee, but if it's job-related, your firm will probably pay it.

◆ | Buy a Book

Bookstores are great places to meet men. Some bookstores, especially those that focus on special topics, such as the occult, murder mysteries, or science fiction, have reading areas where one can have a cup of coffee and browse through the books before deciding which ones you want to buy. These places are ideal for meeting men since the stores want their customers to get to know each other.

Often the proprietor greets customers and has conversations with them. Join in. Or remark to the fellow glancing through a book in a soft chair by the window, "Is that Johnson's latest?" People come to these kinds of bookstores because they want to talk to people as well as select books. He wants to meet you!

In general bookstores, the best times to meet men are during lunch on a work day, in business areas, or on Saturdays, if it's in the suburbs.

◆ | Develop an Interest in Film

A surprising number of men are fascinated by photography. When they're not out taking pictures, they can usually be found in photography stores looking at the latest equipment. So why not stop by the store and browse?

If you see someone interesting, obviously ask him a question, such as, "I'm thinking of buying a tripod but I can't decide which one I ought to buy." Almost any photographer can talk for at least half an hour on that subject!

When you spot a man out taking pictures whom you'd like to meet, ask him about his equipment. Something like, "What sort of lens is that?"

Maybe he'll even take your picture and then drop by your place to give you a copy? Or invite you over to his darkroom to see what develops?

◆ | Walk Your Dog

If you live in an area where there are a lot of men but you never get a chance to meet them, walk your dog. Or borrow a friend's and walk that pooch.

Try to do it on a regular schedule—say six o'clock

every weekday afternoon. That way if one of the men has been wanting to meet you—or sees you and wants to meet you—he'll know when he should "accidently" bump into you.

Since most men love dogs, it's easy to meet them. If you should, for example, spot an interesting man washing his car, stop and watch. He'll probably pat your dog on the head. Once he touches your dog, smile and say hello. Dogs make conversation easy since you can always talk about them.

◆ | Visit the Physical Therapist

Treating your lower back pain, or even taking your friend's son to see about his football injury, may be your key to romance.

Although all sorts of people are treated by physical therapists, therapists who specialize in sports injuries see a tremendous number of men. These days with so many men working out, jogging, playing tennis, etc., there are a lot of men getting injured and receiving therapy on their doctors' orders.

The best place to meet these men is the physical therapist's office—in the waiting room or in the group treatment room. Obviously, since most of these men hold regular jobs, they make their appointments for Saturdays and for after working hours.

The editor of this book can personally attest to the success of this method. One of her most exciting relationships came about thanks to a bout of tendonitis!

◆ | Sail Away on a Freighter

If your soul responds whenever you see an old Humphrey Bogart film and you wish they still made men like the characters he used to play, despair no more. They still do.

But you normally won't find these men in the United States. They and their European and Australian counterparts prefer more remote areas of the world. Third World countries where cargo hauling ships dock. If you take a cruise ship you'll never meet them.

A freighter is a ship that carries cargo from one port to another along with a few passengers. It's nothing like a cruise ship, for it has no swimming pool or live orchestra or movie theaters. Freighters are working ships and the passengers they carry are just a special kind of cargo.

But you will have a cabin of your own and you'll certainly have no problem becoming acquainted with the other passengers. And you'll probably be invited to take your meals with the ship's officers. One of them may be just your type.

When you dock in a remote port, you're likely to encounter some fascinating men. I met one on a tropical island once. Who knows who you may meet?

◆ | Collect for Charity

In most office fund drives, nobody seems to want to go around and collect for the United Fund or whatever. So you should speak right up and volunteer. Make sure you're given an assignment where you'll be talking to people you normally never meet. That is, if you work in the Marketing Department, volunteer to collect in Production or Personnel.

Not only will you meet all kinds of new men, but you won't have to come up with anything original to say if you don't want to. Just talk about the charity.

This same principle holds true for neighborhood fund drives. Volunteer to collect for the Heart Fund or the Cancer Society. It'll give you an excellent opportunity to meet the men who live in your neighborhood.

◆ | Go Househunting on the Weekend

If you live in or near a major city, there are a number of new housing developments being built especially for singles and childfree couples. You'll know them by their ads. And they aren't just looking for the young either. They're also after the divorced and the widowed.

You can meet men at such places, but you don't have to buy a unit. Just find a model you feel reflects your taste and sit down on the sofa in the living room and wait. That way anyone who comes to see the model will run smack into you. Visitors will think you work there or have some other good reason for sitting there.

If a potential Mr. Right should walk in, flash him a charming smile, shrug, and say, "I'm trying this model on for size."

You could end up buying the place together.

◆ | Browse in a Lumber Yard

Many men seem to just love the touch, smell, and heft of wood. And they love to make things out of wood. To cut and to hammer it. So on weekends lumber yards are full of men having a sensual time checking out the stacks and stacks of lumber.

Maybe you should join them.

A comfortable way to meet a man who interests you is for you to have already picked out some woodworking project from a book. Such books are for sale at lumber yards. That way you can approach the fellow and ask, "Can you help me? I'm planning to build a bookcase, but I can't decide what sort of wood I should use for the shelves."

He'll probably give you all kinds of advice and even help you pick the wood out. He may even fall in love with you on the spot since his favorite fantasy is to meet a woman who loves to build book-cases just like he does. Really.

It's a nice hobby and while you're looking for just the right man, you can furnish your house with furniture you made yourself.

◆ | Volunteer as a Tour Guide

Many museums and historic old homes or buildings that are open to the public cannot afford to hire staff to conduct guided tours, but they usually welcome volunteers who are willing to conduct tours for no pay.

It's pleasant work, it serves a good purpose, and the staff there will be very appreciative. All you have to do in the way of preparation is to read a book or two about the old structure. They'll be available for sale right there at the entrance.

And you'll meet practically every man who comes in: the out-of-town male who's visiting, the newly-moved-to-town male, and the men who live in your city and are showing their guests around.

◆ | Jog

Whether it's in the park at sunrise, along a suburban street after breakfast, or on the beach in the soft oranges and pinks of twilight, jogging is a good way to get in shape and to meet men.

Now that the designers have come out with all kinds of great fashions for joggers of both sexes and all ages and builds, everyone can look great.

Since jogging is usually done when other more sedentary mortals are at home, a spirit of camaraderie prevails that makes meeting men very easy.

◆ | Speak Up

It was a bright sunny day. As the good-looking young woman walked slowly past the man leaning against the sportscar, she said in a low, pleasant voice, "Nice car you've got."

When she didn't get the response she had hoped for, since he merely said, "Thank you," in a polite tone, she casually kept walking and smiling.

Although she didn't realize it, he wasn't really alone, for I was with him, but I was ten feet away buying a couple of ice cream cones.

Yet nobody was offended—least of all him. He was flattered, of course. I thought she had good taste in men, and she realized he was taken. But no harm done and it certainly was worth a try.

So if it suits your personality, by all means give any man who interests you an opportunity to meet you. Just say something nice and friendly to him. At any time. Any place. The elevator. Gas Station. At a stop light. Anywhere.

I've never known a man who wasn't flattered— even if he wasn't available. So if he doesn't pick up on it, just assume he's married or engaged so your ego won't be wounded.

◆ | Visit Your Own Hometown

Maybe you should become a tourist in your own city. A fun, and often free, way to meet men is to visit public attractions that offer tours for visitors.

Is there an old gold mine in your area, an astronomical observatory, a dam across a river? They probably offer tours in the summer, and if you go, you can meet men who are visiting your city as well as local divorced dads who have taken their children on an outing. Abandoned windmills, railroad stations, army forts, old public buildings—all are excellent places.

The best way to find out about these attractions is to get hold of informational brochures that are put out by your city. They are available at hotels, motels, and car rental places, and explain what the attraction is, where it is, and when it's open.

◆ | Find Kindred Spirits

If you are a religious person and want to help others find the peace you have found, volunteer at your church to do religious canvassing.

Although Sunday morning is a common time to

go, Friday evening is actually better. A man who doesn't have a date and is home on Friday night might just enjoy talking to you regardless of his religious interests. Obviously any man you meet who is interested in your message will have something very important in common with you. In fact, you might want to invite him to go to church with you on Sunday morning.

• | Visit an Auto Supply Store

Since auto supply stores are such male domains, it's possible you've never even noticed all the ones that are around. So if you can't think of any offhand, check the Yellow Pages.

Many men have ongoing love affairs with their cars. They buy them gifts at the auto supply store. Things like seat covers and pop-up moon roofs. Special waxes and polishes.

Go in any time—but especially Saturday afternoon—and you'll find yourself surrounded by men!

• | Tour the National Parks

Backpacking or camping out in remote areas, such as in some of our national parks and forests, will give you an opportunity to meet men who relish the great out of doors.

Even if you're not up to sleeping under a tree or hiking forty miles with a heavy pack on your back, the national parks are good places to meet men. The more remote or unusual parks, such as Everglades National Park in Florida with its alligators, attract serious nature lovers you can easily meet on the carefully laid out nature trails.

You don't have to stay overnight, but you may prefer to stay at one of the comfortable lodges the park service maintains. That way you can attend the evening nature talks and meet the handsome rangers as well as your fellow lodge guests.

◆ | Eat Fast Food for Sunday Dinner

A good number of the people frequenting fast food places for the midday meal on Sunday are divorced fathers with their kids in tow. It's his visitation day, but dad doesn't like to cook. Plus he hates to clean up afterward, and the kids prefer hamburgers anyway. So why bother? Dad doesn't.

But he's probably dying for some adult company and conversation—and he's certain to welcome a woman who likes his kids.

If you're not shy, just walk up to his table—your tray in hand—and say something like, "Mind if I join you? I just love kids and I don't have any of my own." Sure he may be surprised, but if he had a woman he cared about in his life, she'd probably be eating right there with him and his kids so it's certainly worth a try. Besides he's bound to smile and nod.

A lot of divorced fathers have a hard time making small talk with their children since they aren't aware of their day-to-day activities, so if you really are good with kids, he'll certainly notice and like you for it.

If you're a little shyer, why not start a conversation with one of his kids—in line, at the napkins, whatever—and let dad use that as his opportunity to say hello to you if he wants to.

◆ Fly Alone

Whether you're traveling for business or personal reasons, you shouldn't miss the opportunity to meet someone on the plane. But not just any man —the one you want to meet.

The best way to do this is to arrive at the boarding area more than a half hour before your flight is scheduled to depart. Since almost all seating assignments are given out these days in the boarding area, all you have to do is sit within hearing distance of the check-in counter and wait.

If a man who interests you checks in, you'll hear the attendant tell him his seating assignment. Let's say it's seat 16A. Now you get into line. When it's your turn to select a seat, simply request the seat beside the man you want to meet by saying, "16B, please."

◆ | Tour a Factory

A number of manufacturers in your area probably welcome the public and offer scheduled, guided tours of their plant facilities. These tours usually last from twenty minutes to a couple of hours. Not only are they interesting, but visitors are sometimes given generous samples of the finished products.

Each tour is interesting, and they all attract men. If there's a car manufacturing plant near you, you'll very likely be given goggles to wear as you watch the raw metal body parts being assembled, welded, and painted. Normally children under ten aren't allowed on these tours, but if you visit a dairy or an ice cream manufacturer, you'll see lots of young children accompanied by their divorced daddies. These dads also like to take their kids to baking companies and food processing companies.

Tours of newspapers are interesting, as are brewery and winery tours, especially since they frequently offer free beer or wine to their visitors after the tour.

It's very easy to meet a man on any tour since the atmosphere is informal and the group of visitors meanders about.

◆| Study Navigation

Some things, for a variety of reasons, just seem to interest men more than women. One of them is navigation.

If you live near the sea coast, near one of the Great Lakes, or on a river, chances are good that courses are being taught on navigation for boat owners.

Don't worry about not owning a boat. After all, you should know how to navigate before you buy one, although it's true that many men don't.

Call the Coast Guard, a community college or junior college, or the State Police and make inquiries about what courses are being offered. Or ask around the local marina.

You may be the only woman in the class!

◆| Enjoy Japanese Food

Many Japanese restaurants have teppan-style tables where the food is prepared right in front of the guests. Six to eight guests are seated around each chef at these sort of table-grills, and the guests are encouraged to talk to one another and to the chef while he works.

Conversation couldn't be easier—just talk about the marvelous food and the showmanship of the chef, who'll be flipping the food into the air and dicing everything in sight. A good time to go there is at lunch, for that's when businessmen like to eat there.

Some Japanese restaurants also have sushi bars, which also encourage interaction between diners. In many of these you sit at a sort of counter as the food passes you on dishes on a conveyer. Just take whatever you want as the food slowly moves past you. You pay at the end of the meal when the hostess totals up how many dishes of each color you have before you.

• | Learn a Bit from a Byte

Men love machines and computers are machines. Men seem to love to control things and computers were made to be controlled. Men love computers and they love talking about them.

So on a Saturday afternoon why not make a list of the computer stores in your area, visit them and talk to the other customers—almost all of whom will be men.

You don't have to know anything at all about computers to visit a computer store. Many people who walk in admit they don't know anything but they want to learn. Don't believe any stories you've heard that computers are hard to use. If you understand how a typewriter and a file cabinet work, that's all you need to know.

So ask any male customer you want to meet any question at all. Something like, "Do you like this one?" Or, "Do you know how to operate this?" He'll show you!

If you end up fascinated by the computers as well as by the men and purchase a computer, join the computer club for that brand. The store will explain how to join. Probably all the other members of the club will be men!

· | Go Hunting

Whether it's birds or big game, there's something in carrying a rifle or a shotgun and going after dinner that appeals to some men's sense of their own true self. So the best place to meet these fellows is to go hunting yourself.

This is one occasion when trailing along with a brother or your dad won't hurt your chances of meeting men.

But it's important that you not be the type who flinches at the idea of killing an animal. If you think of deer as sweet, spotted animals with chocolate brown eyes, this one isn't for you. Comments like that from you will only annoy a hunter and turn him off to you. If you can't be proud of what you bagged, don't go. It'll only sicken you.

But if you do choose to go, you'll probably find yourself outnumbered by guys ten to one. Not bad odds!

◆| Attend a Reunion

Just because someone didn't fascinate you the first time you knew him, doesn't mean he won't look better the second time around. So don't pass up an opportunity to attend any sort of reunion.

But try very hard to leave your false pride at home. Don't pretend all evening that you are so popular, so busy, so successful, that you haven't the time or the interest to get to know any of these men. Even very popular women enjoy meeting new men.

Reunions are even better if they're not your own. If one of your girlfriends is invited to a reunion, tag along. Since you'll stand out by being the only woman no one used to know, the men will probably flock around.

◆| Eat Breakfast Out

Breakfast is an excellent time to meet men. With the hectic pace of modern life, many men, especially the unmarried ones, drop by a restaurant or fast food place for a quick breakfast on a weekday.

Plus men who are traveling have to eat breakfast out, and breakfast business meetings are becoming more common all the time.

So almost any coffee shop, restaurant, or fast food place near hotels, businesses, or shops is likely to have a good share of men in it in the early morning. In big cities, hotel restaurants are especially good places to meet successful businessmen.

◆ Trade Houses for a Few Weeks with a Stranger

Trading houses is an excellent way to have a marvelous and inexpensive vacation and meet scores of interesting men.

And it's very simple to arrange. All you have to do is advertise your home, or apartment, with one of the associations that specializes in house swapping. Pictures and descriptions of the houses for exchange appear in the directories that these associations sell.

So you pore over the directories, looking for just the right house in just the right spot. Matching up is quite easy actually since you normally write directly to the other owner and make all the arrangements.

Let's say, for example, that you agree that for the last two weeks of August they'll live in your big city apartment and you'll live in their quaint country home in a little English village (if Englishmen are your cup of tea).

But what about meeting the men after you arrive? Easy. Since the people in whose house you'll be living have already told all their friends and neighbors all about you and that you are coming, you'll probably be swamped with invitations to dinner, garden parties, and tea.

And you can—with perfect propriety—go around and introduce yourself to anyone else you'd like to meet.

If you just want to take an inexpensive look at what's available, you might want to contact the Vacation Exchange Club in Youngtown, Arizona. Its directory lists over 6,000 homes all over the world. Lots of them in England.

• | Open a Savings Account

Have you ever had the feeling when you go into a bank that you've suddenly become invisible? It is frustrating and confusing, but it's also an excellent opportunity for you to meet a man.

Whenever you go into a bank or savings and loan, look around. Is there an attractive man sitting by the potted palm with an exasperated look on his face waiting and hoping someone, someday, may take notice of him and help him?

Misery loves company, so go over and commiserate with him about how confusing everything is while you take a nearby chair.

Banks frequently take so long transacting routine business, you may have the opportunity to have a nice twenty minute chat.

You won't just meet lawyers at a law library. You'll also meet law students, a number of whom will be businessmen who are working to earn law degrees part-time. Plus you'll meet men from all walks of life who are handling their own law cases. These men are usually bright and articulate and very determined to see to it justice is done for them.

There was a time when it was difficult for average citizens to use law libraries, but that's changing rapidly. Computers and librarians have now made it much easier for people to find cases and to understand how legal procedures work.

How do you find the law library? Since they're near law courts, ask a law clerk at the courthouse where it is. Or just phone the courthouse and ask.

Law libraries are set up very much like regular libraries with the walls lined with bookcases filled with books and the center of the room taken by tables and chairs.

Every informed woman should know about laws that pertain to her, so the first time you go in, ask the law librarian how to look up information on a specific legal topic that interests you. For example, the laws governing inheritance in your state.

How do you meet him? Ask him a question, of course. Not a legal opinion. An information question that usually works is, "Do you know where the law books for other states are kept?" They're usually in a separate area. Or you can ask, "Do you know how late the library is open tonight?"

◆ | Try the Martial Arts

It's mighty handy to be able to defend yourself, and practicing the martial arts will also keep (or get) your body toned up.

Judo and karate are subjects that mostly men are interested in, so you may discover that all the other students in the class are male.

The defensive skills you learn can be very useful, and if you enjoy it, you can go on and on in it and meet all sorts of male devotees.

◆ | Sell Him

If your way of earning your living allows you flexible hours, you might want to consider meeting men by taking a part-time job during the day leasing and selling commercial real estate.

You'll be selling and leasing office and industrial space to professional men, such as architects, dentists, and doctors, and to businesses. You'll meet lots and lots of men and have the opportunity to drive them around to see properties you have selected for their inspection. You'll be able to spend plenty of time with them and find out a myriad of things about them and their businesses.

A big plus is that the men you meet will see you as a professional like themselves. You can also make lots of money, although there is a downside: all the money you'll earn will come from commissions.

You'll need a real estate license, but don't panic. They're not hard to get. Call up your state's real estate department and ask them exactly what is required. You'll probably have to pass a written test, but there are books and classes available to help you. The Society of Industrial Realtors also sponsors introductory classes on commercial real estate sales. Honestly, it's not hard to get a real estate license. I have one myself.

◆ | Go to Swap Meets

Lots of people like to get a bargain. And some people enjoy the challenge of trying to get the price down. If you enjoy such things, look around and you'll probably discover three or four places near you that hold swap meets on a regular schedule, such as on the first Saturday of the month.

They usually advertise in the local papers and there's often a permanent sign prominently displayed in the parking lot, on school grounds, in the park, what-have-you, where the swap meet is held.

Drop by. Usually no admittance is charged to buyers, for only sellers pay. Then wander around and look at the wares and the men selling them and the men looking at them.

If you see someone interesting, walk over, and make a comment about what he's selling or what he's thinking about buying. It's as easy as that, for it's a relaxed, informal atmosphere where conversation comes easily.

• | Visit a Headhunter

No, I don't mean an executive recruiter. I mean a real headhunter. If you're the sort of woman who loves adventure and excitement—and men who are adventurous and exciting—you can take trips to remote corners of the earth with like-minded people —mostly men. Go to exotic places like the Sepik River country of New Guinea, where the guides warn you that some of the people are still cannibals!

How do you find out about these trips? There are tour companies that specialize in taking small parties into remote, desolate, and dangerous areas. You can talk to a travel agency about these companies or you can contact them directly to find out what sorts of trips they're offering. These firms advertise in magazines devoted to science, natural history, or archaeology.

The men who are attracted to these trips are not really Indiana Joneses. More often they're very successful entrepreneurs, high ranking executives, independently wealthy men, professionals, or creative types like painters or writers.

One word of caution: These trips can be very expensive. But you'll probably have a once-in-a-lifetime experience and maybe meet a once-in-a-lifetime man.

◆ | Golf Alone During the Week

If you enjoy golfing and can get away during a weekday, consider going to a busy golf course and asking to be put into a foursome. Of course, since the club prefers that anyway, they'll probably put you in a foursome whether you ask or not.

The other three players will probably be men. If it's Wednesday afternoon, maybe doctors.

Try playing on different days at different starting times at different courses and you'll probably meet a lot of interesting men.

Even if many of the men you meet and play golf with are married, a number of them will probably mention you to their single brother-in-law or to their buddies.

◆ | Visit the Race Track

Since lots of men love to win—especially when they're betting on horse or dog racing—going to the track is a good place to meet these men. Who knows, you may bring him luck!

You might prefer to go when well-advertised special races are being held, for the crowds are bigger and the state of excitement and anticipation makes it easier to get into a casual conversation.

But it's always easy to meet a fellow at the track. Just ask, "Who'd you bet on?" He'll not only tell you, he'll probably tell you why.

◆ | Go Fishing

You may love the peace and contentment many devotees find in fishing. Plenty of men like it.

Since you can fish just about anywhere there's water, you'll usually find men on any public fishing pier, bridge, or beach. They'll be standing there—alone—with a pole in their hands contentedly watching for a bite.

Just walk up to him and ask, "Are they biting?" Who knows? You may end up volunteering to cook up his catch for dinner at your place.

◆ | Take Him for a Ride

Could you use some extra money? How about a part-time job driving attractive men around while you talk to them and get to know them?

All you need to know to be a taxi driver is how to drive, how to speak English, and how to find your way around. If you're not too familiar with your city, buy a map and study it for a couple of days before applying for a job.

When's the best time to work? Friday evenings are good, for that way you'll meet many professionals and businessmen who are going to the airport to catch a flight home or arriving back in your city after a week away.

And, of course, Sunday evenings and Monday mornings are also great times, for that's when the in-town fellows leave and the out-of-towners arrive. But actually any time's a good time if you work at the airport or in the business and hotel district. Around dinner time on any business day, you'll encounter a lot of men going out to dinner.

Since talking to taxi drivers is a long established American custom, you won't have any problems getting a conversation going, but use the opportunity to your advantage. If he interests you, see to it he notices you. For instance, you might want to mention early on what you normally do. Something like, "Although I'm really a kindergarten teacher, I drive a cab at night."

◆| Join Professional Associations

The sort of work a person elects to do to earn a living is usually a good indicator of many other things about that person's personality. So people with the same kind of job often have many other things in common. Which means you'll probably like men who do the same thing for a living that you do.

The easiest way to meet these men is by joining an occupational organization. Whether it's the American Medical Association, the American Marketing Association, or the Society of Philatelists, they all hold conventions and conferences. If you go —and it's usually tax deductible—you'll meet men from all over the country who are likely to have a lot in common with you. Men who will want to get to know you.

Some associations and societies allow nonmembers to attend their conventions and conferences for a slightly higher fee than members. So if males from a particular profession interest you, you might consider attending their conventions so you can meet a lot of them.

How do you find out about associations? Go to the reference section of the library and look up the field you're interested in in the Encyclopedia of Associations. There you'll find its name, address, phone number, and description. Call them and find out how to join or ask if nonmembers can attend meetings.

Or ask people in the profession what associations they belong to.

◆ Go for the Gold

No, I'm not suggesting you begin training to win a Gold Medal in the Olympics. But maybe you'd like to win an athlete for a boyfriend?

Whenever there is a major sports event with visiting athletes, people just like you are needed to help out as hostesses, chaperones, chauffeurs, guides, whatever. And wherever the athletes are temporarily housed, staff is needed to assist them and to make sure things run smoothly.

Some of these positions pay a salary; most are filled by unpaid volunteers. You could be such a volunteer.

Phone organizations that sponsor such events and inquire about their staffing needs.

◆ Learn to Ride a Horse

If you're looking for someone like a Marlboro man, you really should learn how to ride a horse. It isn't hard and right along with the riding lessons you'll usually learn how to corral the animal, clean its shoes, and put on its saddle and bridle.

Armed with all this information you can try riding in some pretty exotic areas populated by some rugged outdoorsmen. Almost anywhere there are riding trails, horses are for rent. You can even cross the Continental Divide on horseback in a small group. That's the sort of trip that would appeal to an outdoors-minded male. Don't worry—a paid cook, usually male—is part of the group.

But you needn't go so far as the Continental Divide. Just riding in rural areas near the major cities will give you plenty of opportunities to meet men. And don't overlook bridle paths in parks.

◆ | Get Interested in Local Government

Many people are not interested in local government so unless there's a crisis brewing very few people usually attend city council meetings. But the people who do attend are usually men. What sort of fellows? Frequently men thinking of running for public office or men already involved in politics or the law. So why not drop by the next meeting and see if any of them are your type?

In the suburbs the meetings are usually held in the evenings, one or two times a month. Bigger cities hold theirs in the daytime. Call your city hall, and ask when and where they're held.

◆ | Be a Kid Again

It's a wonderfully clear Saturday afternoon with a fresh coat of clean white snow on the ground and you'd like to meet a man. Where do you go? To the nearest open area that has a high hill, carrying a large piece of cardboard under your arm, naturally.

This is sledding and tobogganing weather at its best. But what men can you hope to meet? Divorced fathers who take their children tobogganing on their visitation days.

You can approach him directly by saying, "It's nice to see a man spending time with his kids."

◆ | Teach a Course

You don't have to have a lot of degrees or be famous to have a skill or talent that others would enjoy learning from you.

Community and junior colleges and high school extension programs are looking for people to teach classes. Perhaps your skill is a hobby like ceramics, gourmet cooking, or painting landscapes? Or maybe you earn all or part of your income from it, such as real estate, accounting, or gardening? Whatever it is, you'll probably love teaching it.

So call the schools and colleges near you and ask to talk to whoever's in charge of extension courses —or maybe they call them summer courses or night classes or a host of other names, but they'll know what you mean. Then don't be shy, volunteer to teach a class.

Will you get paid? Almost always! Will you meet men? Of course! All kinds of men. Not just the ones who take your course either, but the male instructors at the school and the other male students as well as the administrators.

A good place to meet men is to go along with your students to the cafeteria during the class break for a snack. They'll introduce you to everyone!

• | Get Your Hands Dirty

Would you like to do something extraordinary? Perhaps go on an archaeological excavation or help with a monkey census in Africa?

Don't worry, you don't need a lot of special training to do adventuresome things. You'll learn as you take part.

If it's archaeology that interests you, it's best to start on a local archaeological excavation such as a nearby Indian site, but you can instead elect to do something quite spectacular such as helping to dig up Carthage in North Africa.

The way to get started is to call your local university and ask to speak to the Anthropology Department. They'll know all about what excavations are being conducted and which ones are seeking volunteers. Or write to the Archaeological Institute of America in Boston, which serves as a clearinghouse.

I have never met anyone who didn't enjoy being

involved in "a dig." Male amateurs usually outnumber females, while about ninety percent of professional archaeologists are men. A word of caution though—archaeologists live simply, so you may be housed in a tent and food may be cooked communally over an open fire, but age is no barrier.

If other kinds of scientific research expeditions interest you, contact Earthwatch, the Boston-based field research organization. They sponsor expeditions every year all over the world, from Greece to Tahiti. All sorts of professional men spend their vacations working on Earthwatch projects.

No, you won't get paid. In fact you'll have to pay your own transportation and expenses—but it is tax-deductible.

• | Take Up Skydiving

Parachute jumping may not have been your girlhood dream, but if the idea at all interests you, consider for a minute how many men enjoy the sport. It's really a man's sport. Recently divorced men seem to especially enjoy it, and that's a nice time to meet a man.

You don't have to be a participant to meet the men, either. Instead you can be a spectator on the ground when a competition is being held among skydivers. Many men interested in the sport go to these competitions and will be milling around right beside you.

If the idea of taking a lesson intrigues you—remember the class will usually be all male except for you—you can usually find out information about schools at local airstrips or look in the Yellow Pages under "Parachute Jumping" of course. The first lesson usually lasts half a day and ends with your very first jump from a plane.

Don't worry about buying equipment, for jump schools supply all the necessary equipment.

Jumping from a plane is unlike anything you've ever tried!

• | Be Patriotic

Every once in a while in any city the American military will sponsor some special attraction. It may be a free tour of a visiting battleship or submarine or a fly-over by the Thunderbirds (who fly fighter planes in precision formations). Whatever the event is, it'll be designed to attract men of all ages and it will!

No matter what the attraction is, from moon rocks to aircraft carrier, you'll easily be outnumbered ten to one by the men.

Since these events are heavily advertised on radio and in the newspapers and mentioned on television, they're easy to find out about.

◆ | Steak Him Out

Men who live alone usually eat lunch out on Saturday. But they don't just eat anywhere. Somehow they find each other. So why don't you join them?

These men, who prefer counters in coffee shops, don't just order their food and eat their meals in silence. They talk to each other and to the waitress behind the counter. They sort of take the place over in a nice kind of way.

Do a little prospecting. Between 11 A.M. and 2 P.M. on Saturday pay a visit to a number of coffee shops that have counters. You know, the kinds of places with tables and booths that also have counters. You'll know instantly if you've found a "live one," for eight to ten men will be sitting at the counter talking back and forth.

An important reason they're there is because they're lonely. So sit down and join in the conversation while ordering lunch. You'll probably find a stool right in the middle of everything because the men have a tendency to leave empty stools between them even though they're talking. They'll be delighted to have you join them.

◆ | Express Yourself Artistically

If you enjoy being creative and you'd like to meet some creative men, consider expressing yourself through art.

That is, take group painting lessons. Art supply stores usually offer them as do private teachers, colleges, and sometimes galleries.

The size of the group is usually six to ten. Since the classes are small, it's probably best to check out the various classes you hear about before deciding which one to enroll in. Just drop by a class meeting and look over the instructor, the techniques, and, of course, the men.

Men often enjoy painting because it allows them to express a side of their nature that they may otherwise keep locked away, the poetic, sensuous side.

◆ | Sing, Sing, Sing

Do you love to sing? Would you like to meet a fellow who loves it, too? Why not join a chorus, a choir, or a barbershop quartet (yes, in these liberated times females can belong to them!).

If you can't find a singing group that interests you after checking the churches and civic groups and local colleges, call some voice teachers and ask them for recommendations.

If you join a group, you'll not only meet the men in the group, you'll also have the opportunity to meet male members of the audience.

◆| Talk to the Animals

Almost every city has a zoo. Almost every divorced father takes his kids to the zoo at least once or twice a year. So the zoo is a great place to meet him.

Saturday or Sunday afternoon is the best time. The apes and monkey area is the best place. Kids love watching the antics of these furry little creatures.

Elephants and giraffes are also popular with children, as are koalas, if the zoo has them. A special children's petting zoo is also very good.

Once you've picked out the man you want to meet, how do you meet him? Make contact with one of the children first. You could say to his little boy, "Isn't that monkey cute? Do you think you could swing like that from a tree?" Once you start a conversation with his child, dad will just naturally join in. Remember, he wants to meet you, too.

◆| Take Pictures

Everyone seems to love photographs—especially ones of themselves. So if you don't know your way around a camera—but you'd like to—take a course or read a book, but get acquainted.

Once you have the knowledge and a good camera, tell all the people you know—don't forget the gang at work—that you just love to take photographs and you'll be happy to take pictures for them of any event they're going to have. Such things as baptisms, weddings, bar mitzvahs, parties, graduations. All of these are great places to meet men.

Taking pictures allows you to talk to anyone. You can walk right up to that distinguished stranger with the graying sideburns and ask him to smile. Then you can have an extra print made up for him and send it to him with a little note from you the following week. Or you can boldly drop by his place and give him the print in person.

◆ | Try Scuba Diving

If you've ever snorkled and enjoyed it, you might love scuba diving. But you have to take lessons, and that's when the fun—and the men—begin.

Stop by any diving shop or scuba store and all the customers are likely to be males. It's here where you can talk to enthusiasts—they love to talk about the sport—rent some equipment, and take a group lesson if you're interested.

After that, whenever you go on a dive, you'll meet lots of men—men who'll really like the fact you're interested in their favorite sport.

◆ | Get Active in Civic Affairs

No matter where you live, there usually are local problems that need local citizen involvement. Perhaps your city needs a beautification program or a crime-watch program? Maybe the drunk driving laws need changing? Or a new dam ought to be built? Or a highway or a hospital?

Get involved. Have Sunday brunches to air the issues. Or organize Thursday night open discussion groups. Or Saturday night fund raisers. Since anyone who might be interested can be invited to these events, it gives you a marvelous opportunity to call up any man you want to meet and invite him to come.

If others hold meetings or parties or events regarding this matter, attend and speak up. Clearly state your name and your point of view. Afterward a number of men will come over to meet you, since many of them will agree with your viewpoint and will want to express their support.

◆ | Putt Him In

Public golf courses usually have putting greens where golfers can practice their putting on warm, sunny days. You'll find it right next to the club house, and wonder of wonders, there's almost never a fee for using it. On a nice Saturday or Sunday you could meet a lot of men at such a place.

You don't even need a reservation. Just show up and start putting.

Don't worry, you don't need to wear golf shoes or to own a set of clubs. Just wear something flat, like tennis shoes. You do need a putter and a ball. Since putters are sold separately from sets of clubs, you can buy an inexpensive one at any sporting goods store, or get a friend to lend you one.

And don't worry if you don't know how to putt. You know the idea is to gently hit the little ball into the hole. Practice will give you the precision and concentration that's called for.

It's best to call the golf course first—they're listed in the Yellow Pages—and ask them if they have any rules regarding the use of the putting green. Also ask when it's busiest, for that's when you want to go!

◆ | Collect Toys at Christmas

Would you like to help underpriviledged children have a happier Christmas while meeting lots of caring, concerned men at the same time?

Every year before Christmas, groups of men get together to collect toys for children who otherwise wouldn't get any. These toys are wrapped and distributed to needy families and to children in public care.

Fine, family-oriented men get involved in these projects. Some of them are single and don't have children yet, while others are divorced fathers whose children live far away from them, and there are others whose children are grown up.

Since fraternal associations are often involved in these efforts, this is an excellent way to meet men who belong to these normally men-only type of voluntary associations.

Why not get involved and give them a hand? They need people to pick up the donated gifts, to sort and wrap them, and to deliver them to the parents of the children.

◆ | Plan a Trip

Maybe you'd like to arrange a charter plane trip to Europe? By organizing it and selling all of the seats, you can get your fare paid.

Not only will you get a free trip, but you can use the trip as the perfect opportunity to contact men you'd like to meet. You can phone high school teachers and professors at colleges and universities, tell them about the charter flight, and see if they might want to buy a seat. Find out their names and telephone numbers from directories, such as the ones that all universities and colleges put out. Most of these directories also indicate if the man is married by listing the name of the wife—if there is a wife.

If a man you phone sounds interested—and interesting—offer to meet with him and discuss the charter in more detail.

♦ | Eat Lunch in the Park

When the leaves turn to gold and crimson and brilliant scarlet and are about to fall, there's no place like a park—especially if you work near one that people like to stroll around during the lunch hour. On a nice autumn day hundreds of people will be sauntering about at noontime.

So pack a very attractive picnic hamper—take along extra dessert—and enjoy your lunch from a bench that is so close to the path that a man need not leave the path to sit down next to you.

If a man who does interest you sits down beside you, turn to him with a smile and say, "Isn't it a lovely day?" Then offer him some dessert.

♦ | Meet the Police

Would you like to meet some of your city's finest? No, you don't have to rob a bank or get mugged to meet a cop.

Policemen are easy to meet in an informal way, because they have a habit of "hanging out" at donut shops late at night.

Look in the phone book for open-all-night donut shops and then drive around and look for police cars parked out front. Midnight and later is the best time to go. You'll probably spot at least one police car at every donut shop.

78

Look in the window, as if you're looking at the delicious goodies, and size up the men in blue. When you spot a man you'd like to meet, go inside and ask him for the thing you can ask any policeman on earth for. Directions. It's as easy as saying, "Hi, Officer, I'm trying to find Hennepin Avenue." Or, if you're a bit bolder, "Hi, I'm Sally Forbes, and I think I took a wrong turn."

Make good eye contact and thank him when he says, "Take a left at the corner and go three blocks."

But don't leave. Order a jelly donut or two and something hot to drink and sit down with him and his buddies and chat for a bit.

Don't worry about what to talk about. He'll ask you where you're going, and you can ask him how long he's been on the force.

Remember, one of the reasons he became a policeman is because he likes to help people.

◆| Shop at Convenience Stores

Convenience stores like 7-Eleven know that their customers are mainly single people of all ages. And they want their stores to be nice places for singles to meet each other.

That's why they sell coffee and sandwiches—so singles will stay awhile and chat. There's no pressure. The stores are set up so you can wander around, which makes it very easy to take a look at the other customers.

A dear friend of mine met her boyfriend when she stopped by such a store at nine one night for a quart of milk and some donuts. Since the donuts came six to a package, she approached the attractive man she wanted to meet and asked him if he'd like to split a package. Indeed, he did!

◆ | Join a Barter Club

Many people enjoy getting something for nothing, although, of course, when you're bartering it's not really for nothing. You are trading something you have for something they have. In barter clubs people often trade services, that is a lawyer trades his services with a doctor. Or people trade goods such as a pair of skis for a bike. Since men particularly like barter clubs, when you join one you'll meet plenty of guys.

Don't worry if you feel you don't have a skill or item to barter, for you probably do but don't realize it. Do you bake delectable chocolate goodies that everyone raves about? Make homemade wine? Perhaps you sew? Whatever it is, once your name and phone number are in the barter book, you'll start getting calls. But why wait? Make some calls of your own to the men that are listed!

◆ | Visit a Dinosaur

Since even before Charles Darwin's time, men have been fascinated by natural history. They are intrigued by the birds and beasts of the woods and plains. Captivated by the mammals and fish of the deep. If you've never looked into it, why not give it a try? You'll meet plenty of men.

Although you may never have been there, the city you live in—or one nearby—probably has a Natural History Museum. Just call the information operator and ask for it by that general title. Then drop by.

If the subject turns out to interest you, consider volunteering to help out at the museum. They always need volunteers. Who knows? You may be put in charge of unpacking dinosaur bones. Think of all the men who'd stop by then to talk to you and to ask questions!

Also look into scientific expeditions that the museum sponsors or is affiliated with in some way. They'll probably have a listing of the local scientific expeditions posted near the entrance. You're going to meet all kinds of men if you go along on one of these. It may be a nature walk along the ocean. Or a chance to see the whales migrating south. Or a visit to an excavation unearthing prehistoric animals. You won't even have to be gone overnight. Sign up. Give it a try.

♦ | Swim on Over

Call the schools and YMCA in your area—or in the area where you'd like to meet a man—and find out which ones have community pools. Inside pools are the best. Then find out what hours the pool is open to the public.

Divorced fathers take their children to the pool, because it's an activity they can enjoy together on the day they visit him.

So put on your suit and jump in.

Meeting people, as you know, is easy in a pool. But if you're a bit shy, meet his children first. Then his son can do the introductions. "Hey, Dad, this is Janet."

♦ | Attend Craft Fairs

So many people are interested in handicrafts these days that even the shopping malls are holding craft fairs in their interior courtyards. And parks often sponsor them, as do civic groups, schools, and churches.

They are a good place to meet men since the atmosphere is relaxed and cheerful and the crafts-people and their wares are right there so there's always a topic of conversation available.

If you feel too shy to talk directly to the man you'd

like to meet once you're standing beside him, ask a question instead of the craftsperson. If you ask a general question such as, "Why does this interesting cup have three handles?" the man you want to meet can easily join the conversation—and he probably will.

◆| Exercise Your Dog

There seems to be something about watching a dog running free and chasing a ball or a stick that attracts some men like a magnet. So if you have a dog you can trust off a leash, take your pooch to the park for a play session.

In my experience, men who are attracted to dogs who are off-leash are different from men who are attracted by dogs on leashes who are docilely walking beside their owners. This sort of man responds to the sense of freedom and unpredictability of the dog being only under your voice command.

How do you meet him? When you notice him watching you and the dog, holler out and ask him if he'd like to throw the stick. You bet he would! And he may also want to wrestle with the dog.

These men are playful and fun loving!

◆ | Go to Court

Some men aren't content with merely watching court cases dramatized on television. They want to see the real thing. You'll find them in the spectator area of the courtroom while court is in session.

Different sorts of men are attracted to different sorts of trials. While one man may watch two or three divorces before lunch on his day off, another fellow may prefer seeing criminals tried for their lives. So sit in the various courtrooms and experience the atmosphere of each while you take a look at the type of male spectators there.

You certainly don't need anyone's permission to watch a trial. All you do is walk in and sit down in the public area in back. Conversations are easy to start since you can always whisper a comment to him about the case.

◆ | Take Pen in Hand

Do you have a yen to be a writer? Do you read newspaper articles and find yourself wishing you'd chosen journalism for a career? Or maybe you just like the idea of covering a story and being in on things.

You can do it and you can meet lots of men doing

it. And you don't need training as a journalist either! What you need is burning desire and enough spunk to go out there and get the interview and the story.

Who are you going to interview? Every attractive man you encounter? Sounds like a great idea!

How do you get started? In your neighborhood or community there is probably a "throw-away" newspaper or a "shopper" or a weekly that doesn't have a large circulation, but covers stories about the community you live in.

It certainly can't afford to hire you and pay you, but go, in person, to visit the editor and ask what kind of stories he or she "might" be interested in publishing. Then go find such a story and write it and submit it. Be careful to cover the who, what, where, when, and how.

Better yet, have an idea in mind for a story when you go to visit the editor. Suggest the story and offer to write it and submit it for consideration. The editor might be willing to agree to "take a look" at it. If that happens, you're a reporter. You're writing on assignment!

You can now interview any man about anything. After all, the paper might publish your story about him.

And you now have a wonderful, never-fail, opening line for meeting men. "Hi, I'm a reporter for . . ."

◆ | Seize the Moment

You now know a lot of fun, interesting, and natural ways to meet just the kind of men you want to meet. And lots of 'em! Someday, however, you may suddenly see an attractive man you really want to meet, but the situation isn't covered in this book, and you have only a moment or two before he'll disappear forever.

Times like when you spot a man waiting for an elevator or for an attendant to bring him his car. Or maybe he's walking through a hotel lobby.

No matter where you are, don't miss your chance. Make contact by asking him for one of two things. Which one you ask for depends upon the circumstances.

Ask him either, "Do you have change for a dollar?" or "Do you happen to have a postage stamp?"

Either way you'll get his momentary attention. If he wants to meet you, the next step is his.

A Concluding Word: Double Your Pleasure— and Your Chances

As you put into practice the recommended ways to meet men, you're going to be meeting lots and lots of men who are just your type. Wonderful and special men who want to build a relationship with you.

And as the love and romance and commitment you've always wanted, and so richly deserve, flow into your life, you're going to gain a new perspective of yourself. You're going to have increased feelings of self-esteem and self-confidence. After all, now that you've taken control of your own fate and are actively seeking what you want, you're the person you've always wanted to be.

But for all these marvelous things to happen, you have to lead with your right foot. It's not hard, it's very easy really, but you may have formed a habit in the past of unintentionally leading off with your left foot.

You want the someone special you've met to discover how wonderful you really are. Bear in mind that ninety percent of what he thinks you're like will be based on the opinion he forms in the first half hour or so that he knows you. It's hard to change first opinions. Too hard! So don't make it necessary.

Don't let yourself down by starting off with pessimistic or negative remarks about yourself or your life situation. Consider for a moment these two possibilities.

Girl meets boy she likes. Boy likes girl. Girl tells him about herself by saying, "I've got two kids, no support money, a job I hate, and loads of bills I can't pay." Boy thinks, "What a drag!" and leaves.

Okay. Now, same boy, same girl, but this time girl says (also equally true), "I go to college nights and belong to a computer club. I'm interested in fishing (how she met him) and horseback riding, and I'm planning to take up golf." This time he thinks, "Wow, what an interesting woman!" and stays.

Obviously, it would be equally bad to start off with, "I've been seeing a married man, but he's gone back to his wife and I'm so lonely." Or, "I just got fired and I'm about to be evicted from my apartment."

Save the negative, unhappy aspects of your life—and everyone has them—until later in the relationship when you know each other better. That way he'll be able to understand how the downers in your life fit into the general picture. By telling him all the bad stuff first, you're actually misleading him—unless you only have bad stuff in your life.

Don't mention your children, if you have any, right away. (Do not, however, lie about them if he asks.) Yes, I know they're wonderful, but very few men are looking for instant families. Let him know you first. Let him find out what you're like as a person. There's plenty of time. He may have children, too. But at the beginning focus on the two of you—as people, not as parents.

What sorts of things should you tell him about yourself when you first meet him? Never make things up. You don't want any man you have to impress with phony stuff. You want to present the real you—but in a positive framework. Good topics are a job you love, goals you have and the progress you're making toward them, hobbies you enjoy, and any of the suggested ways in this book that you've tried or are planning to try. Most of the recommended ways to meet men are interesting things to do and fun to talk about. Obviously, don't mention all the guys you've met doing them!

What shouldn't you tell him right off? Don't put your former boyfriend or ex-husband down. This new fellow might be someone's ex! Don't put anyone down. Don't complain about money or other problems you're having. Don't whine and ask for pity.

Be positive and keep smiling. Smiling actually

makes you feel better as well as making you look prettier. So have a good time and enjoy the experience of getting to know him and telling him about you.

Just relax and introduce the wonderful, special, and unique woman you are to the hundreds of men you're going to meet who are just your type.

How to Make The Best Use of This Book

After you've read the book through, select five or ten recommended ways to meet men that attract you. You'll probably choose ways that fit your present interests and lifestyle.

When you try them out, you'll immediately begin to meet lots of men who interest you and who are interested in you.

But don't stop there. Branch out and try some of the recommended ways that are challenging and make you personally try new things. That way you'll meet new kinds of men. Just as importantly, you will grow and experience parts of yourself that you never even knew were there!

You're involved in a fascinating, exciting adventure. You're on a marvelous treasure hunt.

Good luck!